LET'S FIND OUT

A Picture Science Book

by Nina and Herman Schneider
Pictures by Jeanne Bendick

PUBLISHED BY WILLIAM R. SCOTT, INC., NEW YORK

LET'S FIND OUT

Library of Congress Catalog Card No. 46-3175

HOW TO FIND OUT

If you dropped a heavy stone and a light stone together, which would reach the ground first?

Three hundred years ago a man named Galileo did just this. He found out that what happened was entirely different from what everybody expected. Everybody expected the heavy stone to reach the ground first. But it didn't. Galileo tried it over many times, and each time both stones reached the ground at exactly the same time.

Some people refused to believe it. They said the stones were bewitched.

Others went home and tried to find out for themselves. They took all kinds of light and heavy things: a piece of wood and a piece of stone; an empty box and a full one; and any two things that didn't just drift through the air. Each time the same thing happened. The light and heavy things reached the ground together.

Galileo was a scientist. He did a simple experiment with two stones. What he learned is true. It is as useful and true today to a man who designs elevators or airplanes, or bombs, or pile-drivers, as it was to Galileo long ago.

There are many experiments you can do for yourself to find out about things that you want to know. You don't need great telescopes or huge engines. With simple things you have in your own home, this book will help to show you how to find out some interesting things about heat, weather and air.

HEAT, THE MAGICIAN

The jam jar cover is stuck. You can't get it off, hard as you try.

Run hot water over the cover of the jam jar for a few minutes.

Take the jar away from the water. Now the cover comes off easily.

WAS something sticky washed away from the lid?

What did the hot water do to the lid of the jam jar?

LET'S FIND OUT

GET a clean, dry empty jar with a screw top.

DO THIS. Turn the cover on so tightly you can't open it easily.

Run the hot water over the top until the cover is hot.

Turn the cover. It opens easily now.

You used a clean jar, so there was nothing sticky to wash away. Something else must have happened to make the cover looser.

Did the cover get bigger when it was heated?

The cover looks the same, but it loosened.

LET'S FIND OUT

What happens to metal when it is heated?

GET a piece of thin bare wire. (A single strand of picture wire is good.) A screw driver. A kitchen chair with a back. A candle.

DO THIS. Tie one end of the wire to the screw driver, about one inch from the tip of the blade.

Tie the other end of the wire to the top of the chair back, so that the screw driver blade is just under the bottom rung of the chair.

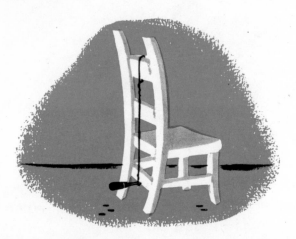

Now hold the lighted candle half way up the wire. (The wax will drip on the floor, so put a plate underneath.) The candle heats the wire. You will be surprised to see the screw driver handle dip down because the wire slowly grows longer.

Now remove the candle. Sit back and watch the screw driver ride up slowly as the wire cools and becomes smaller and shorter.

Try it a few times. You will see that the heat makes the metal wire get bigger each time. When the wire cools off it gets smaller. And the screw driver rides up and down.

Now we can try the jam jar again and see that the heat made the metal lid of the jar get bigger and looser.

WE FIND that heat makes metal get bigger.

LET'S FIND OUT

Do other things get bigger when they are heated?

GET a weather thermometer (or a bath or cooking thermometer) and two dishes.

DO THIS. Look at the thermometer. See how the liquid fills part of the tube. Notice at what number the top of the liquid is.

Fill one dish with hot water and one dish with cold water.
Dip the thermometer in the hot water.

Keep it there one minute, or until you count slowly to sixty. Watch the liquid get bigger and go up in the tube. To what number did it climb?

NOW, DO THIS. Dip the thermometer into the dish of cold water.

Keep the thermometer there one minute. Watch the liquid get smaller and shrink down into the bulb. To what number did it fall?

WE FIND that when the liquid in the thermometer is heated it gets bigger. When it is cooled it gets smaller.

Now we know that metal is not the only thing that gets bigger when heated. Most things get bigger (*expand*) when heated and smaller (*contract*) when cooled.

DO YOU KNOW THAT

—Sections of railroad track are laid with open spaces about so big | | between them? This leaves room for the tracks to stretch on hot days without doing this:

Next time you ride on a train listen for the clicking as the wheels pass over the spaces.

—Cement sidewalks are made with cracks like those in the picture? You can feel them as your skates click over them. Why are the cracks there?

—The great Empire State building bends a little on a hot day because the sunny side expands (*gets bigger*) more than the shady side?

—Even a huge heavy thing like a steel bridge expands (*gets bigger*) when it is heated and contracts (*gets smaller*) when it is cooled? On a very hot day, the long steel cables that hold up the bridge become longer than they are on a very cold day. You don't see the bridge move up and down. The bridge moves slowly, because the weather changes slowly. But the bridge does move.

If you were a magician and could command the weather to change from very hot to very cold, you could give yourself a nice ride on the George Washington Bridge in New York City. Its cables shrink eight feet and up you'd zoom. Cold and hot, up and down.

HEAT MOVES WITHOUT FEET

You feel warm in bed. You take your blankets off. You feel cool.

You lie in the warm bath. After a while, the bath water cools.

You feel hot in the sun. You go in for a swim. Now you feel cool.

WHERE does heat go when something cools off?

LET'S FIND OUT

GET a cup almost full of hot water and a silver spoon.

DO THIS. Set the spoon in the hot water. Hold the tip of the spoon handle. Feel the heat come into your fingers.

Some of the heat from the water moves into the cool spoon.

The heat moves out of the water, up the spoon to the very tip.

Then the heat moves into your fingertips.

Now can you see how the end of a pot handle can get very hot, though the handle is not touched by the fire under the pot?

If you don't use a pot holder, the heat from the handle flows into your fingers. And that hurts!

WE FIND that heat moves.

Heat moves from things even when they aren't very hot.

LET'S FIND OUT

Will heat always move out to anything that is cooler?

GET a small piece of ice and a coin.

DO THIS. Put the coin on the piece of ice. Watch it melt a round place in the ice.

The coin isn't very warm, but it's warmer than the ice.
So the heat moves from the coin into the ice and melts it.

Have you ever warmed your mittens on a radiator?

Some of the heat from the warm radiator moves into the cold mittens. Then, when you put them on, the heat from the mittens moves into your cold fingers and your hands feel warm.

When you put on your mittens and make snowballs, the heat leaves your mittens and moves into the cold snowballs.

The heat from your warm hands moves into the mittens and your hands feel cold.

WE FIND that heat always travels from warm things into colder things.

You feel **cold** when heat travels **away** from you into something else.

You feel **warm** when heat travels **into** you from something else.

DO YOU KNOW THAT

—Heat flows from the fire into the pot, when you are cooking food? Then the heat flows from the pot into the food.

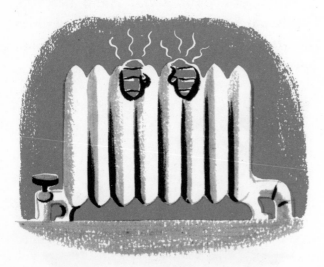

—When you leave ice cream on your plate, the heat from the room flows into the ice cream and melts it? Then the room becomes just a little bit cooler.

—When you leave hot soup in your plate, the heat from the soup flows into the room? The soup gets colder, and the room gets a little bit warmer.

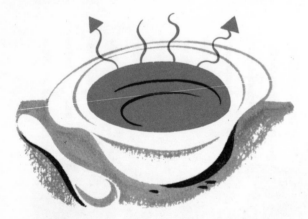

—When you put food into the icebox, heat flows from the food into the ice? The ice melts and the food is cooled.

—Heat from the sun makes the beach sand hot? When you walk on the sand, the heat goes into your feet.

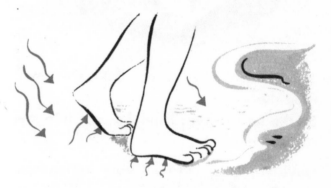

—When you pour water on a fire, the fire is put out because the heat flows into the water? No matter how hot the water gets, it won't catch fire.

HEAT TRAVELS FAST OR SLOW

It's morning. Time for you to get out of your nice, warm bed.

When you go into the bathroom, your feet feel cold on the floor.

Hop on to the bath mat. You will find that your feet feel warm.

WHY do your bare feet feel warmer on the mat than on the floor?

Now put your right foot down on the mat.
The foot on the floor feels cold.
The foot on the mat feels warm.

LET'S FIND OUT

DO THIS. Stand with both bare feet on the bathroom floor.

Can it be that you have one cold and one warm foot?

Try it the other way.   Put your left foot on the mat.
The foot on the *floor* feels cold.
The foot on the *mat* feels warm.

LET'S FIND OUT

Does heat travel faster through some things than through others?

GET a saucer, a sock, and two ice cubes.

DO THIS. Put one ice cube on the saucer and one ice cube on the sock.

Hold the saucer on one hand and the sock on the other hand. Which hand feels colder?

WE FIND that the hand with the saucer feels colder.

Heat flows from your hand through the saucer into the ice cube, faster than through the sock.

The saucer is like the tile of the bathroom floor.
The sock is like the bath mat.
The tile floor carries the heat away from you faster than the mat can.
The foot on the floor is losing heat fast.
It feels cold.
The foot on the mat is losing heat slowly.
It doesn't feel so cold.

Now, let's try something else.

GET one ice cube, one wooden match, a nail about as big as the match.

DO THIS. Hold the match in one hand and the nail in the other.
Press them both against the ice cube.

—A package of ice cream will stay cold longer under a pillow than on a dish on the table?

—An ice cube in a mitten will keep colder than an ice cube left unwrapped?

Which feels colder?

The metal nail feels colder than the wooden match.

WE FIND that heat runs away faster through metal than through wood.

Why?

Because heat travels faster through some things than through others.

—The hair on a dog is like a blanket? Long haired dogs are clipped in the summer because long hair holds the heat in the dog's body like a blanket.

—Blankets of various kinds are built into refrigerators to keep out the warmth? These blankets, called insulation, are also built into walls of houses.

—An aluminum cup and a plain china cup can be used in an interesting experiment? (Fill each cup with very hot water and then touch the handles.
Does heat flow better through aluminum than through china?)

—On a cold day the metal door knob feels colder than the wooden door.

—Metal ice skate runners feel colder than your leather skating shoes.

—Handles of radiators, electric irons, and toasters are usually made of wood.

Do you know why?

HEAT WORKS FOR YOU

The rain makes puddles so big that you can sail a boat in them.

At noon, the puddle is smaller. The boat is almost grounded.

Later in the day, the water dries and the boat is high and dry.

WHAT makes the water dry out of the puddles?

You have seen other things that dry out. Grass that is wet early in the morning dries up in the warm sun.

After swimming you stand in the sun to dry.

Water dries out of a kettle that has been left heating on the stove.

Wet clothes in the sun dry faster than wet clothes in the shade.

Heat must have something to do with drying.

Does heat help water dry out of things?

17

LET'S FIND OUT

GET two pie plates.

DO THIS. Put one full tablespoon of water in each pie plate. Put one plate on a hot radiator and the other in a cool place.

Wait a few minutes.

WE FIND that water will dry out in a warm place before it dries out in a cool place.

LET'S FIND OUT

Will more heat make the water dry faster?

Pour out water left in the pans.
Put two tablespoons of water in each pan.
Put one pan on the table and one pan on the lighted stove.
Wait for the water to dry out.

WE FIND that more heat makes the water dry faster.

LET'S FIND OUT

What happens to the water? Does it just disappear or does it go somewhere?

GET a small saucepan.

DO THIS. Put half a cup of water in the saucepan. Set the pan on the stove. Light the fire. Soon the water will heat.

Watch the bubbles come from the bottom. As soon as bubbles form, the water is boiling. First you see little bubbles form, then bigger and bigger ones. They explode when they reach the top, and send little puffs of water up into the air.

The singing you hear in kettles is the noise of bubbles forming and exploding. The little puffs of hot water are called steam.

Soon the hot fire makes all the water boil away. Now turn off the fire.

WE FIND that great heat makes the water steam up into the air.

LET'S FIND OUT

What happens to the steam or water drops? Do they just go away, or are they still in the air?
Can we bring them back?

GET a teakettle with a spout, and a cool, dry, empty milk bottle.

DO THIS. Put half a glass of water in the teakettle and boil the water.

Watch for steam to come out of the spout. Take the dry, cool bottle and hold it over the spout. (Not too close—the steam is hot and can burn your hand.)

Watch the little puffs of steam stick together to form small drops of water. When enough drops join they become heavy and roll down the side of the bottle.

Watch for the little trickle. Feel the bottle get warmer and warmer. Put it down before it gets too hot.
What has happened?

As soon as the hot steam touches the cool glass, the steam turns back into water.

WE FIND that when water is heated it goes up into the air as steam.

WE FIND, TOO, that when the steam is cooled, it turns back into water and falls down.

—The steam heating system in the house works like a steaming teakettle and a cool milk bottle? (Study the picture below for an explanation of how heat works.)

The warm milk bottle at the top is like a warm radiator. The spout of the tea kettle is like a steam pipe. Steam in the spout is like steam in the pipe. The kettle is like a boiler and the water in the kettle is like water in the boiler. The gas stove is like a furnace.

This is how heat works for us.
The heat from the furnace fire turns the water in the boiler into steam. The hot steam rises in the pipe until it reaches the cool radiator, and warms it. Then the heat from the radiator travels into the cool room. The room is warmed.

MAKE YOUR OWN WEATHER

The fog is thick. Boats whistle and hoot to each other through it.

Autos have headlights lit and crawl along slowly in soft mist.

Windowpanes are wet. Streets are lit early. Fog sits over the city.

YOU can make fog yourself. What is it?

LET'S FIND OUT

GET one clean empty milk bottle and one piece of ice large enough to rest on top. (If your ice cube is too small, take two and squeeze them together. They will freeze into one big piece.)

DO THIS. Pour a glass of hot water into the bottle. Rest the piece of ice on top. Hold the bottle in front of a strong light.

Watch closely to see what happens.

See the warm damp air rise. It meets the cool air under the ice and the tiny drops of warm water in the damp air are cooled.

When the warm moist air meets the ice, real fog forms. What you see swirling up and down the bottle is fog.

You have made fog.

21

When it rises a little higher off the ground, we call it fog.

The warm water in the bottle is like the water in the lakes and rivers, which the sun warms.

The ice is like the cooled air when the sun is not shining.

The fog in the bottle is just like the fog on the rivers, roads and cities.

WE FIND that when warm moist air is cooled, fog forms.

Warm moist air that has been cooled is called different things as it rises.

When it rises a little way from the sun-warmed ground and settles on the grass and flowers, we call it dew.

When it floats up into the sky, we call it clouds.

Clouds float in the sky until something happens to them.

You already know what happens when warm moist air is suddenly cooled.

LET'S FIND OUT

What happens when the cloud is cooled?

GET a teakettle, and a small saucepan.

DO THIS. Put one glass of warm water in the teakettle and boil the water. Fill the saucepan with very cold water. When the steam comes out of the spout, hold the saucepan so that the steam hits its side. See the cooled steam form drops of water that come pattering down the side of the saucepan like rain. You have made rain!

The cloud is like the steam coming from the kettle. The steam is cooled by the cold saucepan, the way the cloud is cooled by the cold air.

If you could cool the air suddenly, you could be a real rainmaker, anywhere, even in the desert. For even over the hottest desert, there are sometimes clouds which form rain when they are cooled.

WE FIND that when water is heated, it rises into the air as steam, or fog or clouds. After it is cooled in the air, it comes back down again as water.

All the water that rises, comes back, rises, and comes back over and over again.

DO YOU KNOW THAT

—"Dew" forms on the walls and mirror of your bathroom when you take a warm bath or shower?

—Frost forms on the windows when the moisture in the room is frozen by the cold glass?

—A little fan blows hot air from the motor up against the windshield in most automobiles, in order to keep frost from covering the windshield?

—The wetness on cold water pipes is formed like dew on the grass in Summer? The cold pipe makes the nearby moisture in the room cool off and form drops of water on the pipe. Some people mistakenly think that these drops of water come from inside the pipe. They say the pipe is sweating.

These are the names we call moist air that rises and falls: dew, fog, clouds. The picture below shows them all at their proper levels.

These are the names we call moist air that meets freezing weather and falls: snow, sleet, frost. The center of the picture shows rain falling from a cloud.

RAIN

SNOW

SLEET

FROST

AIR! IS IT REAL?

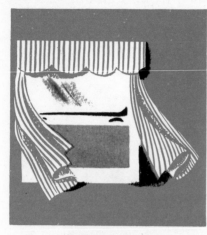

The curtains blow in at the open windows. Why?

A bird glides by without moving its wings. How?

A leaf turns as it drifts slowly down. Why?

AIR, air, air.
Air, all around.
Airplanes and birds fly through the air.

But you can't see air. You can't hold it.
Air has no color; it has no shape.

Is it a real thing like a door?
A door can close and keep you out.
Can air keep things out?

Is air real like lemonade?
Lemonade can be poured from one glass into another.
Can air be poured?
If it can, it's real.
Is air real?

LET'S FIND OUT

Can air keep things out like a door?

GET a drinking glass. A paper napkin. A large mixing bowl.

DO THIS. Nearly fill the mixing bowl with water. (A few drops of ink stirred into the water will help you see what happens.) There is nothing in the glass but what is all around us—the thing we call air.

NOW, DO THIS. Hold the glass upside down. Push it down to the bottom of the bowl.

Tip the glass in the water. Watch the bubbles of air come out.

Now tip the glass till all the air has come out and there are no more bubbles.

Keep the glass in the water, but turn it bottom up, like this.

Now lift it slowly until the whole glass is almost out of the water.

The glass is full of water. The water couldn't come in till you tipped the glass and let the air out.

It looks as if the air in the glass can keep the water out.

NOW, DO THIS. Crush the napkin into the bottom of the glass. Hold the glass upside down over the bowl of water.

Push the glass all the way down to the bottom again.

Now lift it out. Don't tip the glass. Take out the napkin and feel it. It is dry!

Air has kept the napkin dry.
Air has kept the water out like a door.

You can't see air because it has no color. But air is real.

Can air be poured like lemonade?

(This is easy to do if you follow the pictures.)

GET two drinking glasses. Use the same bowl full of inky water.

DO THIS. Push one glass under the water and tip it until all the bubbles of air have come out and the glass is full of water.

Then turn it bottom up and lift it almost out of the water.

Now hold the other glass bottom up so that the open end is under the glass full of water, as in the picture.

Tilt the glass full of air and watch the bubbles from it pour into the other glass and push the water out.

The glass that had air in it is now full of water.
The glass that had water in it is now full of air.

You have poured air from one glass into another.
Now try pouring it back the same way.

WE FIND that air is real.

Air has no shape. Air has no taste.
But you can pour it like water or lemonade.

DO YOU KNOW THAT

—When a drop of soapy water is blown full of air it becomes a soap bubble? When the bubble breaks you can hear the puff as the air rushes out.

—It is air that stretches a balloon till it bursts? The bang is air rushing out.

—If there were no air, the raindrops would fall fast enough to smash the sidewalks? But the air slows their fall.

—The ground is full of air? If you pour some water into a glass full of soil or sand you can see the bubbles of air coming up.

—After rain, worms come out of the ground because they need air to breathe? The rain makes the air in the earth bubble out.

—Men can build under the water without wearing any special diving suits? They work inside a large steel tank that is shaped like a tall drinking glass upside down. These tanks are called caissons. The bottom of the caisson is open, but the air keeps the water out, and the men stay dry. An air pump sends down fresh air for the men to breathe.

RIDING ON AIR

The truck looks crooked. What's wrong?

Soft tire. The man pumps air into it.

Slowly, the truck is lifted. Now it's straight.

CAN a soft light thing like air pick up a heavy thing?

LET'S FIND OUT

GET a large paper bag and a book.

DO THIS. Twist the open end of the bag the way you do when you want to blow up a bag to explode it. Put the bag on the edge of the table. Put the book on the bag and blow.

Watch carefully and see the book rise.

Put another book on top of the first one and blow. See how many books you can lift with air. (If you have a balloon, use it instead of the bag.)

WE FIND that air can be used to push up and lift things.

Sometimes a plane, when landing, crashes its landing gear and must be lifted to

31

be repaired. There's no room to get jacks underneath the wings, so big rubber bags are squeezed under and pumped full of air. Up goes the plane just the way the book went up.

The air to lift a truck with a soft tire is pumped by a motor or hand pump. The air to lift the plane is pumped in the same way. The air to lift the book was blown by you.

LET'S FIND OUT

Does air push even when you don't blow or pump it?

GET a drinking glass and a card big enough to cover it. A piece of cardboard from a cracker box will do.

DO THIS. (over the sink, just in case) Fill the glass with water. Hold the card on top of the glass and turn the glass upside down on the card. Now take your hand away from the card.

The card stays on. There is only air under the card. The air must be pushing up.

Now hold the glass sideways. The card stays on. There is only air on the side. The air must be pushing sideways.

Hold the glass right side up. Try to blow the card off. See what a lot of breath is needed to blow the card off.
The air must be pushing down.

No matter how you hold the glass, the card stays on.

Imagine a glass three stories tall and full of water. If you could turn this tremendous glass upside down on a card, the card would still be held up by the air underneath.

Now quickly turn the bottle upside down. The water stays in the bottle!

WE FIND that air pushes even when it is not pumped or blown. It is pushing all the time. It pushes down, up, sideways, and every way.

Just for fun, let's try something else.

GET a milk bottle and a piece of cheesecloth.

DO THIS. Fold the cheesecloth in half. Tie it over the mouth of the bottle, with a string or a rubber band. Hold the bottle under the faucet and fill it with water right through the cheesecloth.

We know that air held the water up. The water just rested on the cheesecloth and on the air in between the threads of cloth.

AGAIN, WE FIND that air pushes up.

DO YOU KNOW THAT

—The air in your bicycle tire is a springy cushion? It holds you and your bicycle up.

—Air pushes up the soda in a soda straw? Your sucking removes the air from inside the straw.

—It's hard to lift your feet when you're walking in the mud? There's very little air pressing up in the mud under your shoes and lots of air pushing down on top of your feet. The slurp-slurp noise is made when air rushes underneath as you lift your feet.

—Air is a very real thing to a man using a parachute? It is the air that pushes against the parachute and keeps it from falling too fast.

34

AIRPLANES

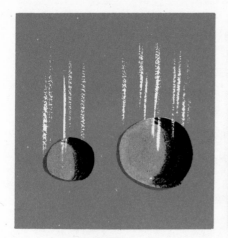

Stones fall fast.

Parachutes fall slowly.

Airplanes don't fall.

WHY don't airplanes fall? What makes them stay up?

Here's a plane waiting to go up.
It has a motor, a propeller, and wings.
The job of the motor is to turn the propeller.

The job of the propeller is to pull the airplane forward.

The job of the wing is to lift the airplane and keep it up.

How does the wing keep the airplane up?

The wing has a top and a bottom. Each does its share of the lifting, each in a different way.

The air under the bottom of the wing pushes up.

At the same time the air on top of the wing pushes down. (We found out earlier that air pushes in all directions.)

The push of the air against the bottom of the wing is as strong as the push of the air against the top. So the airplane stays on the ground.

But if we can make the air under the wing push up with **more** force, and if we can make the air on top of the wing push down with **less** force, the plane will be lifted up and will stay in the air.

36

Can we make the air under the wing push up with **more** force?

GET a piece of paper obout an inch wide and as long as this page.

DO THIS. Hold the paper by one end and pull it through the air like a ribbon.

Watch the flat paper move up and up.

As the paper moves forward, it presses against the air. The air pushes right back and picks up the paper. It pushes back the way a rubber ball or balloon springs back against your hand after you squeeze it. The faster you move the paper, the more air piles up under it and pushes up against it.

A flat thing that is held slanting is pushed up when it moves through the air.

An airplane wing is built flat underneath and slants toward the front.

It is pushed up with more force as it moves through the air.

You pull the paper through the air. The paper rises because the air under the paper pushes up with more force.

The propeller pulls the wing through the air, and the air under the wing pushes up with more force.

WE FIND that we can make the air push up with more force.

LET'S FIND OUT

Can we make the air on top of the wing push down with less force?

GET the same strip of paper you just used.

DO THIS. Hold it at one end. Blow gently along the top of the paper. It flutters a bit, but doesn't rise.

Now blow hard along the top so that the air moves very fast over the top. The paper goes up. It is being pushed up by the air underneath.

But what about the air on top?

Fast-moving air does not push down as hard as slow-moving air. It is so busy rushing forward that it has no time to push down.

You made a wind over the paper. *The propeller,* pulling the plane through the air makes a wind over the wing.

The air **over** the paper **pushes down** with **less** force. The air rushing **over** the wing **pushes down** with **less** force.

WE FIND that we can make the air on top of the wing push down with less force.

When the propeller pulls the plane swiftly through the air, the upward push of air is strong, the downward push, weak. The plane rises and stays up in the air.